The Hell Hawk Poems

By John M. Livingood

Table of Contents

..

Dedication

This book is dedicated to those who fought in World War II and, in particular, to the soldiers and marines that fought in the South Pacific.

Preface

This book is primarily compiled from the records of Dr. William C. Livingood, also known as Doc Livingood. Doc Livingood served as a Navy Lieutenant assigned as the Flight Surgeon for Marine Fighter Squadron VMF-213, the Hell Hawks, in 1943 during the squadron's three combat tours of duty in the Solomon Islands' Campaign. While assigned to the VMF-213, Doc Livingood recorded numerous events and retained certain documents concerning his squadron and the Marine pilots with whom he served.

Doc Livingood's records include his Surgeons' Logs and his flight logs, as well as internal memorandum. Additionally, he collected poems and other documents, including military aerial-nautical maps used by the Marine pilots. While certain operational information is included in the Flight Surgeons Log, its primary emphasis is on the pilots of the squadron, including their condition, both physical and mental. In addition to documenting those lost in combat, the Flight Surgeon's Log accounts for those shot down, or otherwise missing in action and returned, those injured, or sick with malaria, reactions to anti-malaria medications, acute infectious jaundice, dengue fever, acute sinusitis, diarrhea, dysentery, and other miscellaneous diseases. The hardships of combat and environmental conditions, captured in these documents, provide remarkable context for the poems in his collection. These documents and poems allow us to peer through a unique window into the past; a time before television and the internet – a time when men captured their thoughts, recorded events, and creatively expressed their reflections on the world around them through words.

During their combat tours and in the rear, the different pilot squadrons would interact. One encounter that Doc Livingood related involved the aftermath of a "wrestling match" between VMF-213's Milton Vedder and VMF-214's infamous Pappy Boyington. Best recollections of the story have Doc Livingood sewing stitches on Pappy Boyington after the "match." Long after the war, William Livingood received signed copies of Pappy Boyington's books, *Tonya* and *Baa Baa Black Sheep*.

Later, during World War II, Doc Livingood was assigned to marine squadrons VMTB 144 and VMF 514, stationed on the escort aircraft carrier, USS Salerno Bay. Following WWII he was reassigned back to the US Navy and served as senior medical officer on the USS Wright in late 1940s. While in the Navy, he completed his post graduate medical education in otolaryngology at the University of Pennsylvania. He had a notable career in otolaryngology with the Navy where he served as Chief of Otolaryngology Services, US Naval Hospital, Philadelphia, and Head of the National Aural Rehabilitation Center.

Following retirement from the Navy in 1962, Doctor Livingood practiced otolaryngology with the Guthrie Clinic, Robert Packer Hospital in Sayre, Pennsylvania until 1970. For the next six years he practiced medicine at the Veterans Hospital, Fayetteville, NC. He moved to Raleigh, NC in 1977 and served as a medical consultant to the NC Department of Human Resources until he fully retired at the age of 80 in 1995.

William C Livingood, MD, Captain (U.S.N. Retired), died Sunday September 23, 2007, at home in Orlando, Florida.

This publication mainly focuses on the poems collected by Doc Livingood during his assignment with the Marine fighter squadron, VMF-213, and tries to give accurate attribution to the authors to the extent they can be identified. The poems are arranged in three sections. Within each section, they are arranged in chronological order as best can be determined. The first group of thirteen poems, Section A, are those identified with the VMF-213, Hell Hawks; these poems appear to be primarily authored by a Hell Hawk pilot, Theron Hart Brown, III. The second group of eight poems, Section B, are those more generally identified with marines and the war in the Pacific. The third group of four poems, Section C, focuses on the environment and living conditions, including the one and only glimpse of a short Sidney "recreation" tour.

The Introduction will give general context to the Solomon Island Campaign and the pilots of VMF-213 squadron. The introduction contains a separate poem, "A Marine's Prayer," that was not included in Doc Livingood's records but was provided by Sandra Brown, the wife of Sherwood Brown, the brother of Theron Hart Brown, III, and this poem was included in her collection of poems and was noted as being possibly written by Theron Hart Brown, III. Comments are added to individual poems to give additional and more specific perspective and context to those particular poems.

Introduction: VMF-213 and the Solomon Island Campaign

<u>The Japanese Offensive</u>

The Japanese attack on Pearl Harbor was the initial action in a multi-pronged attack. Japanese bombers attacked Guam, Midway, and Wake, as well as Manila and Singapore. The Japanese forces also attacked the Philippines, the Netherlands East Indies, New Guinea and the Bismarck Archipelago. They swept over New Britain, New Ireland, and the Admiralty. Rabaul on New Britain Island was a fundamental part of the Japanese strategy. Rabaul would be their main base of operations from which they hoped to dominate New Guinea, Australia, the Solomon Islands, New Caledonia, Fiji, and New Zealand. By January 1942, they captured Rabaul. The Japanese carrier strike force controlled the seas, and they continued their march southward to strategically-vital Australia; they pushed from Rabaul to Bouganville. In May, they reached Tulagi, capital of the Solomons, and next door to Guadalcanal. Soon an airfield was being built on Guadalcanal.

Two of the Japanese aircraft, often mentioned in Doc Livingood's logs are the big twin-engine Betty bombers, GM4 Medium Bomber, and their fighter aircraft, the Zero, A6M2 through 5 Reisen Zero's. The Zero had excellent maneuverability and range. However, these positive features came at the expense of pilot and gas tank protection.

<u>The Solomon Islands</u>

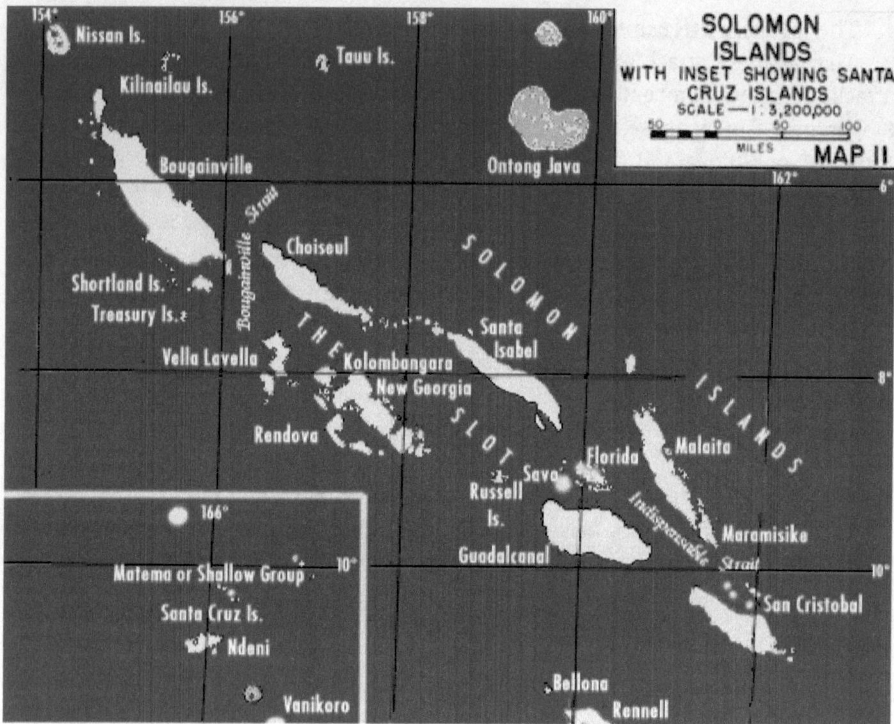

Map from Pearl Harbor to Guadalcanal, History of U.S. Marine Corps Operations in World War II, Volume I.

Although there are numerous islands that actually comprise the Solomon Islands, there are large islands and major clusters of islands enclosing a central passage, nicknamed "The Slot." The Slot runs southeast and northwest. At the top end are Bougainville and Buka, currently part of Papua New Guinea. On the eastern side are Choiseul, Santa Isabel and Malaita; on the western side are San Cristobal, Guadalcanal, The Russells, New Georgia, Rendova, Kolombangara, Vella Lavella, The Treasuries and The Shortlands. In a Central position lays Florida, and to the South is Rennell.

The Slot was a major passage way for Japanese naval vessels during the Solomon Islands' Campaign.

The aerial-nautical maps in the Appendices are copies of the originals from Doc Livingood's collection and were used by the pilots of VMF-213. These maps detail the islands and both the Japanese airfields and United States airfields.

<u>The Solomon Island Campaign</u>

The Solomon Island offensive against the Japanese was but a part of an overall offensive plan stemming from earlier events and designed for a larger objective. In early May 1942, five months after the Japanese attack on Pearl Harbor, the United States laid the foundation for their counter-offensive in the naval engagement, the Battle of the Coral Sea, in which the U. S Navy stopped the advance of the Japanese in their attempt to invade Port Moresby, located on New Guinea's southeastern coast. While the battle itself in terms of ships lost could be viewed as a Japanese victory, it effectively caused the Japanese to call off their Port Moresby amphibious operation invasion and eliminated two of their large carriers, the Shokaku and the Zuikaku, from participating in the Battle of Midway due to damage and air group depletion. One month later in June, the decisive United States' victory in the Battle of Midway further set the path for a land-based counter-offensive.

The Joint Chiefs of Staff's Admiral Ernest J. King is credited with anticipating the Japanese strategic advance southward to New Caledonia, Fiji, and Samoa. He proposed establishing a base at the Island of Efate in the New Hebrides from which a counter-offensive could advance northward to and through the Solomons. In early July1942, the United States Joint Chiefs of Staff issued orders specifying that Rabaul would be taken.

On August 7, 1942, the landing of a Marine division on Guadalcanal and the nearby islands of Tulagi, Gavutu, and Tanambogo began the first stage of the counter-offensive. The initial landings at Guadalcanal went well with little resistance; however, the resistance on the other islands was extremely strong. The fierceness of the fighting on Gavutu inspired the poem, *The Graves of Gavutu*.

In the months that followed, the fighting on Guadalcanal intensified. The Japanese reacted resolutely with air and naval support and with reinforcements to the island. After six months of fighting, Guadalcanal was finally secured in February 1943. Another poem, *Edson's Ridge*, captures one of the more bloody and strategically crucial events, among many, during this period.

On February 21, 1943, the U. S. Army made an unopposed landing on the Russell Islands, 60 miles northwest of Guadalcanal. In addition to naval and air engagements in the ensuing months, the allied forces began the climb up the Solomon Islands. On June 30, the Army landed at Rendova Harbor, and the Marines landed at Viru Harbor. On July 2 and 3, landings were made on New Georgia and at Vangunu Island to the southeast of New Georgia. On July 5, The Marines and Army landed at Rice Anchorage on the Island of New Georgia. The Munda airfield was captured on August 5, 1943. By October 6, 1943, the Central Solomon Islands

Campaign ended with the complete evacuation of Kolombangara and Vella Lavella Islands.

Later in October, the land movements continued to the north Solomon Islands. On October 26, landings were initiated in Treasury Islands. On October 28 Choiseul was invaded.   Finally, on November 1, 1943, the allies landed on Bougainville Island.

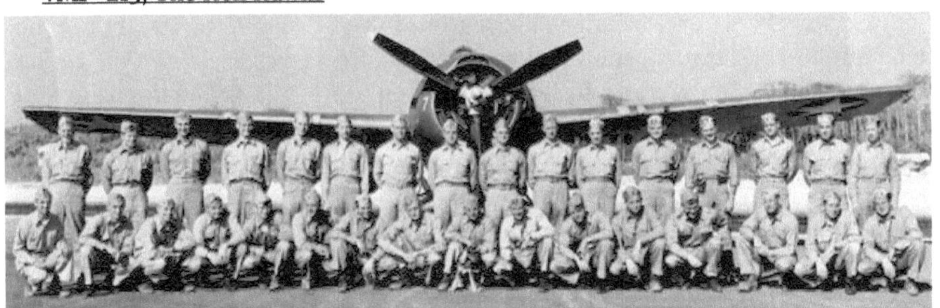

VMF-213 is pictured here at Ewa, Hawaii, on February 13, 1943. A Grumman Wildcat is in the background. Front row: John Thomas(Ground Officer), Walter Hilton, Leland Eckart, William Johnson, Herman Spoede, Wilbur Jackson, Robert Jones, Alonzo Treffer, James Cupp, Foy Garison, Charles Winnia, Edward Shaw, Leonard McCleary, Milton Vedder, Arthur Boag, and Robert Bier (Ground Officer). Back row: Frederick Buechmann (Ground Officer), Sheldon Hall, Gordon Hodde, William I. Coffeen, John Morgan, Milton Peck, Byron Leary, Gregory Weissenberger, Wade Britt, William Humberd, George Defabio, Robert Votaw, Theron Brown, Don Tate, Stirling Harrison (Intelligence Officer), and William Livingood (Flight Surgeon). VMF-213's mascot, Doc Schnauzer, is between Cupp and Garison in the first row.

Marine fighter squadron VMF-213, the Hell Hawks, was formed July 1, 1942 at Ewa, in the then territory of Hawaii. The first echelon of the squadron left Ewa on February 15, 1943, and arrived at Espiritu Santo, New Hebrides, on February 28, 1943. The last three echelons of the squadron arrived on March 8, 1943. Espiritu Santo, New Hebrides, was their rear area of operation.

Squadron designations were based on specific letters used for indicating the missions for each particular type of squadron and its assigned aircraft. As an example, a World War II squadron operating the F4U Corsair aircraft would have been designated a fighting squadron (VF). The letter F, for fighting or fighter, was the key in identifying the type of squadron and was also used in the aircrafts designation. The Letter M would be assigned to Marine squadrons. Identification numbers were assigned to each squadron, hence VMF-213.

VMF-213 were trained on the Grumman built F4F-4 Wildcat. It had four fifty caliber machine guns and was much better protected than the Zero; however it had some severe limitations: lack of power compromised its ability to carry heavier payloads and fuel loads. It lacked the manueverability, power, speed, and ability to climb of the Zero. To compensate for its weaknesses and relying on its strengths, the Marine pilots developed the successful two-plane mutually protecting fight section tactic. However, shortly after their arrival in the Pacific theater, the F4F-4

Wildcats were replaced by the F4U Vought Corsair, giving inspiration to the Poem, *Two-Thirteen and Their F4U's.*

On April 3, 1943, the VMF-213 departed Espiritu Santo, code named both Buttons and EBON, for Guadalcanal, code named Cactus and BEVY. On April 4, they relieved the VMF-124 and started to operate from Henderson Field on Guadalcanal. The squadron's first job was to learn the geography of the Solomon Islands: the islands, the Slot, the location of enemy troop concentrations, the airstrips, etc. Typical missions involved escorting bombers up to Bougainville, a Japanese stronghold in mid-1943, actions against New Georgia, Villa, Munda, Rekata Bay, Vanga Vanga, and Lolabinauri, and included area patrols of the Russell Islands and other surrounding islands.

The Flight Surgeon's Log documents certain operations: beginning on April 4th with local patrols, followed by aerial battles in defense of Russells and Tulagi on April 7th, mission over Choiseul and Kolombangara on April 13th, strafing on Vila and Munda on April 22nd, aerial battle over Vangunu on April 25th, and intercepts in the course of these missions. The first tour ended May 12, 1943, with only two pilots lost and only seven Japanese planes shot down.

The squadron's highly regarded Commanding Officer, Major Britt, died in an operational accident on April 13th. Additionally, Lieutenant Eckart was listed as MIA and never returned. A log entry notes that Eckart "seemed to be straggling in formation" after the aerial battle over Vangunu on April 25th. Later, on June 12th there is a note of an unconfirmed rumor that a pilot was picked up with neck wounds a month earlier and died shortly thereafter, indicating it was probably Lt. Eckart.

The Hell Hawks' second combat tour of duty began on June 17, 1943, and the pace of the war increased dramatically. Combat patrols continued as major land operations began. On June 30th, the squadron engaged in aerial battle over New Georgia and Rendova covering the Rendova landings. On July 11th, there was another aerial battle over New Georgia; on July 15th a large bomber attack on New Georgia was intercepted. On July 17th and 18th, there were aerial battles over Kahili. On July 19th, the Commanding Officer, Major Weissenberger, and Doc Livingood requested Fighter Command to "ease duty on the pilots – no relief in sight for 10 days." After completion of the mission on Kahili on July 26th, all pilots were grounded for "Combat Fatigue." On July 28th, VMF - 124 arrived to relieve the VMF-213.

This picture has been identified as being taken on May 3, 1943, five days before the end of the VMF-213's first combat tour. A Chance-Vought F4U Corsair is in the background. The complement of pilots remained the same for the start of the second combat tour. Front row: D. Tate, F. Cupp, A. Boag, W. Johnson, W. Hilton, R. Jones, F. Garison, G. DeFabio, W. Thomas, C. Winnia, H. Spoede, and G. Hodde. Second row: M. Peck, E. Shaw, J. Morgan, S. Hall, R. Votaw, M. Vedder, W. Humberd, M. Peyton, G. Weissenberger, B. Leary, W. Cloake, A. Treffer, T. Brown, S. Harrison (Intelligence Officer), and W. Livingood (Flight Surgeon). VMF-213's mascot, Doc Schnauzer, is again present.

The second combat tour resulted in 62 Japanese planes shot down. Seven Marine aces were made: Weissenberger, Cupp, Hall, Shaw, Thomas, Morgan, and Vedder. However, the second tour also took a severe toll; six pilots lost their lives: Votaw, Winnia, Garrison, Tate, Peck, and Spoede. On June 29th, Lt. Tate was on morning patrol and had engine failure; he died in a crash short of the runway. On June 30th, Lt. Peck had engine failure and glided to a water landing but failed to get out of the plane prior to sinking. On July 3rd, while returning from combat patrol in late evening, Lt. Spoede "ran into thunderhead" and contact was lost – reported as missing. On July 15th, Lt. Votaw was reported missing, "last seen making a run on a Betty." On July 17th, Lt. Garrison was "shot down in combat over Kahili on return – broke division to make pass at zero . . . shot down, both wing tanks blazing – went straight in not seen to get out." On July 18th, Lt. Winnia failed to return; he was "last seen in combat over Kahili" and was later designated a prisoner of war; he was never recovered. One particular poem, *Over the Horizon*, is significant in that it captures the squadron's pilot losses up through the end of the second Combat tour.

In their third tour, while primarily based on Guadalcanal, the squadron was split-up for periods of time; a significant number of pilots were assigned Munda, New Georgia Island, and, at times, to the Russell Islands. In addition to patrols and escorting bombers, combat actions continued against Kahili and Vella Lavella. On September 12th, a major aerial battle occurred over Kahili; the squadron shot down eight planes. On September the 17th, in an aerial battle over Vella Lavella, the squadron shot down nine planes. On a September 23rd engagement, between Vella Lavella and Kahili, the squadron pilots shot down another 5 planes. By the end of the third tour, another 35 Japanese plane were shot down, bringing the total of Japanese planes shot down to 104 for the Hell Hawks' three combat tours. While no new aces were made, Cupp, Shaw, Thomas, and Morgan added to their tallies of enemy planes shot down: 12, 13 ½, 16 ½, and 8 ½, respectively.

Based on pilot complement this picture was likely taken on between August 26 and September 3, 1943, at Espiritu Santo. A Chance-Vought F4U Corsair is in the background. Front row: B. Ffoulkes, J. Walley, T. Brown, J. Cupp, G. Groom, W. Cloake, J. Anderson, J. Brubaker, C. Toomey, G. DeFabio, F. Avery, W. Thomas, M. Bowers. Back row: L. McCleary, F. Buechmann (Ground Officer), J. Morgan, W. Anderson, H. Huidekoper, W. Stewart, V. Glascock, E. Shaw, R. Foxworth, L. Handschy, R. Roberts, R. Dailey, A. Boag, M. Vedder, G. Bennett, W. Livingood, and S. Harrison. VMF-213's mascot, Doc Schnauzer, is again present.

During the third tour, five pilots were classified Missing in Action and later as Killed in Action: Bennett, Brown, Glascock , Cloake, and Roberts. On Sept. 9th, Lt. Bennett was "last seen in battle near Villa Lavella (in control of airplane)." On Sept. 12th, Capt. Brown was "shot down while strafing Kahili. – radioed 'losing oil pressure', - pulled up to 700 – 1000 ft. and plane went into water – not seen to escape. Time 1730 between Kahili and Shortlands." On September 18th, in an aerial battle over Vella Lavella, both Lt. Glascock and Major Cloake were reported Missing in Action. Glascock was "last seen in run on dive bomber, wing seen to fall off, possibly in explosion, continued down straight into water – guns firing into water." On September 23rd in a battle between Vella Lavella and Kahili, Lt. Roberts was reported down and was last seen in the Shortlands' area.

On October 11, 1943, VMF-221 arrived to relieve VMF-213. That same day, Thomas shot down 3 zeros and 1 probable; Shaw shot down one zero. On December 9, 1943, after their third combat tour and a short rest in Sidney, Australia, the Hell Hawks returned to the United States for reorganization and training.

At the completion of its third tour, VMF-213, the Hell Hawks, accounted for 104 enemy aircraft shot down. The squadron had seven aces based on Japanese planes shot down during the three combat tours: James N. Cupp with 12, Sheldon Hall with 6, John Morgan with 8.5, Edward Shaw with 13.5 (Doc Livingood's log account for 13 ½ planes shot down. Other records record 13 and two suggest 14 ½.), Wilbur Thomas with 16.5 (Doc Livingood's log accounts for 16 ½ planes shot down. Other records indicate 18.5 planes shot down and one record specifically mention two Zeros shot down while stationed on the Essex, an aircraft carrier, in February 1945.), Milton Vedder with 6, and Gregory Weissenberger with 5.

There were twenty-nine pilots as VMF-213's commenced its first combat tour. Eighteen pilots joined the squadron in the course of its three combat tours. Thirteen pilots were designated missing in action and only 3 of them returned. One of the missing in action was accounted as a prisoner of war but never returned. Four were killed in operations.

Ssgt. Coffeen was a pilot that was listed as missing in action but was one of the three that returned.   SSgt. William I. Coffeen's ordeal began with engine trouble during a mission on April 13, 1943, and ended with his return noted in the Flight Surgeon's log as being June 27. The account of his almost three month trek for survival through the islands is not recorded in the Flight Surgeon's log. However, Brian Altobello describes SSgt. Coffeen's ordeal in his book on the battle of New Georgia, Into the Shadows Furious: the Brutal Battle for New Georgia.

In addition to those killed in action and in operations, seven of the original pilots were evacuated to hospitals and never returned to the squadron: Walter Hilton (chronic bronchitis), Robert Jones (tropical ulcer, dermatitis), William Johnson (fracture of left femur), Alonzo Treffer (nausea, abdominal pain, jaundice), William Coffeen (after missing in action for approximately 50 days), Sheldon Hall (fractures and shrapnel), and Francis Cupp (severe burns).

The picture, above, was taken after October 14, 1943, and prior to November 19, 1943, at Espiritu Santo. Front row (left to right): George Defabio, John Luther Morgan, Ed Shaw, Leonard W. McCleary, Milton Vedder; back row (left to right): Stirling Harrison, Ray Boag, Wilbur Thomas, and Dr. William Livingood.

Of the original officers and pilots of the Hell Hawks, the seven pilots, the intelligence officer, and flight surgeon, were the survivors – those that were with the squadron at the beginning of the first combat tour and continued through the completion of the third combat tour. Of the nine squadron survivors of the three combat tours, five survived the war. George Defabio was killed in action over Okinawa on Friday, April 13, 1945. John Luther Morgan was killed in action over Okinawa on March 28, 1945. Ed Shaw was killed in a flying accident near Mohave, California on July 31, 1944. Milton Vedder died on February 11, 1944, in a New Zealand hospital from complications directly related to malaria.

Only, Leonard H. McCleary, Stirling Harrison, Ray Boag, Wilbur Thomas, and Doc Livingood survived the war. However, shortly after the war, Wilbur Thomas was killed in a flying accident in 1947.

The Japanese were not the only enemy in the South Pacific. In summary, the following represents the number of medical cases associated with some of the more predominant medical conditions that afflicted the VMF-213 pilots:

Malaria - 9

Reactions to anti-malarials (atabrine) - 2
Jaundice, acute, infectious - 3
Dengue fever - 5
Acute sinusitis - 7
Diarrhea - 6

Accidents also took their toll in equipment and personnel. There were 20 accidents with injuries: 10 in action and 10 operational. There were nine accidents with no injuries: 2 in action and 7 operational.

Additionally, Flight Surgeon William Livingood, in a retained draft of his Combat Tour Report sent to the Wing Surgeon, pointed out several related operational factors that adversely impacted the pilots. The first was the splitting up of the squadron between Munda and Guadalcanal; the portion of the squadron at Munda being relieved about every ten days. This method of operations resulted in "numerous complaints from all personnel so forced to operate." He believed this method of operations was responsible for "much disorganization, loss of interest, and a much earlier onset of combat fatigue." Secondly, the pilots at Munda were subject to additional adverse situations. There were 34 fighter pilots assigned to Munda but only 14 or less planes were available. All pilots were required to stand ready in the ready tent from 0500 to 1830 each day. There were no days off, the ready tent was a long distance from the camp and mess area, and the ready tent was poorly supplied.

The foregoing tries to account for the conditions under which these marine pilots fought and endured: the hours on patrol and in combat, the air raids while at their own base, the deaths of fellow Marines, injuries on duty, and the myriad diseases, including malaria, jaundice, dengue fever, sinusitis, diarrhea, dysentery, catarrhal fever, and dermatitis. It also tries to capture the spirit of the men who so endured. However, the countless stories of these men, their individual performance, their interaction with the men in their squadron, and their interactions with the pilots of other squadrons are not captured here.

Concluding this endeavor is perhaps best accomplished by an anonymous prayer that was not in Doc Livingood's records but was obtained from Sandra Brown, the wife of Theron Brown's brother, Sherwood P. Brown, and who identified the poem as being written by Theron Brown and contained in the collection of poems in the possession of Theron Brown's relatives:

A Marine's Prayer
Dear God, in a world that's racked with war,
Let me think of the coming years
When the cannon's core has ceased its roar,
And the nations dry their tears.
Keep Thou my heart unblasphemed;

And let me live as a man should live
In a fight for the God of Peace.

O Father, grant that I may last
To build the world again
To know, when pestilence is past,
A brotherhood of men.
Bless Thou the aged with Thy light;
Protect our troubled youth;
  And let me fight as a man should fight
In a war for the God of Truth

Thy will be done, if Thou decree
That I should die afield
But let me go, face to the foe,
Sustain me lest I yield.
Let no man cry he saw me fly
The battle's agony;
And let me die as a man should die
In a fight for Liberty

Section A: Poems Identified with VMF-213

TWO-THIRTEEN AND THEIR F4U'S

The Colonel came the other day,
And took our F4F's away.
The Dutchman cussed and bitched and cried.
"The dirty bums!" the poor guy sighed.
"Our tender care all gone for naught;
and now we've monsters spewn from Vought."
II
His plane mechs griped – and they'd be right-
For each had stolen through the night,
Like bold and hardy crooks of old,
To lift the stuff that Grumman sold.
Both 'Twenty-One and Two-Fourteen
Supplied our band that crept unseen.
III
McLaughlin, Twitty, Dutch, and Barr
Had gathered parts from near and far.
They had equipped us much the best
Of all the squadrons headed West,
But 'twas in vain! For on that day
All Wildcat parts were sent away.
 IV
So there we were a fighting crew,
Gone was the old, and here the new.
Was it true that it stalled out coming in?
Must ya jump if the damn thing started t' spin?
And how about that mile-long nose?
Ours the plane that nobody knows.
V
Complicated! Gadget-ated!
Fleet-winged, swift, and agitated!
Speed and death here concentrated,
To Revenge they're dedicated.
Born to kill – and consecrated
To the task war indicated.
VI
Hot stuff, these planes! A lot to learn,
Studious midnight oil must burn.
"Memorize handbooks! Get the word!

Learn the features!" was all we heard.
Hartsock and Kuhn from 'Twenty-Four.
Taught us a lot of corsair lore.
 VII
The Majors were the first that day
To hit the air the Corsair way.
The whole damn crew had gathered 'round
To cheer or pale as they touched the ground;
To hope and pray that "Ground-loop" Greg
Would keep her straight-no palm tree peg.
VIII
But the wheels hit true, I'm proud to say;
No loops or whirls to mar the day-
Both Britt and Greg smiled down and said
"There's nothing to it. Just use your head."
So all went up to roll and soar,
And thrill to the song of that engine's roar.
IX
The weeks pass by – the hours mount.
An hour a week. Christ! What a count!
Lack of parts- but no lack of rain.
Blood and guts! Who wouldn't complain?!
Treffer and Tate have hit the drink.
All hands give thanks, they didn't sink.
X
Only the start has here been told.
The Tale will grow as the year turns old.
Maybe I'm wrong and maybe I'm right,
But I say we'll win each time that we fight.
As a betting man, the team I'd choose
Is Two-Thirteen and their F4U's.

Guadalcanal April 4, 1943
Brown

<u>Comments:</u>   This poem was identified as written by Theron Hart Brown, III, by numerous sources: it was typed on a sheet of paper with "Brown" written at the bottom; it was handwritten into Doc Livingood's log and specifically attributed to Theron Hart Brown, III; it was contained in another collection attributed to Captain T. H. Brown, III; and Sandra Brown, the wife of Theron's brother, Sherwood P.

Brown, identified the poem as being written by Theron and contained in the collection of poems in the possession of Theron Brown's relatives.

The first US Navy F4F-3 was flown on 20 August 1940, powered by a Pratt & Whitney R-1830 engine with 1,200 horsepower. The subsequent F4F-4, incorporating several improvements including folding wings, six guns and self-sealing fuel tanks, was delivered in November 1941. It was then that the name "Wildcat" was first given to the F4F. As war raged around the world, the Wildcat's reputation and utilization grew immensely. It flew with the US Navy and US Marines in all of the major Pacific battles, and in North Africa with the Navy.

F4U was a single-engine aircraft. The fuselage was round with a small bubble canopy and a tall rounded fin. Fuselage extended past the fin. A radial air-cooled engine was mounted in the nose and was fitted with a four-blade propeller. Low-set wings were inversed-gullwing shaped. They were elliptical with rounded tips. An oval air intake was housed in the leading edge of the wings close to the fuselage. Machine guns were mounted in the wings.

The F4U was an extremely dangerous plane to Japanese pilots increasingly dependent on the Zero design as the war moved on. Its inverted gull wing produced a low drag profile, and the Pratt and Whitney R2800 delivered massive horsepower at altitudes most other planes couldn't reach. A Zero pilot faced in the F4U a plane that was considerably faster, had twice his horsepower, could climb much better, was much better armored, and featured the staple American gun configuration of multiple 50 caliber machine guns with lots of ammo. Not surprisingly the F4U generated a massive (11:1) kill ratio rivaled only by its R2800 cousin the F6F, Hellcat. The Corsair was such a solid design it was used well after the war into the 1950's in a variety of roles.

In early February 1943, the VMF-124 was the first in the South Pacific theater equipped with the Vought F4U Corsairs, the "Bent-Wing Bird" to the Marines and "Whistling Death" to the Japanese. The Corsair had real performance superiority over the Japanese combat aircraft and much greater range than the F4F. Within three months, all eight Marine fighter squadrons in the Solomons were equipped with the Corsair. VMF-213 received their first Corsair on March 9, 1943. Lts. Hartsock and Kuhn of the VMF-124 were temporarily attached to the VMF-213 to help with the training on the F4U.

Thought while riding the Tontouta Aviation Express:

Why are these god-damned bases
Always in the lousiest places?

ORDERS FOR TWO-THIRTEEN

Where the mud is up to the hub caps,
And the jeeps are skidding free,
We will send the fighting young pilots
Of Squadron Two-One-Three.

Where the rain and muck are the thickest,
And the Heavens open up,
Let them pitch their tents 'neath the palm trees –
Let them slither, slather, and slup!

If there's ever rain in the tropics,
And it's dry where they might be;
We must rush these lads to the scene, Boys!
Faithful mud-caked Two-One-Three!

Let their laundry soak in the drying,
Let them sink knee deep in loam.
Always send these lads to the mud-holes;
And, by God! Don't send them home!

Guadalcanal, April 6, 1943.
Brown

<u>Comments:</u>   These two poems in one rendition are on the same page with date, location, and have Brown's name written on the page, thus, helping to identify both poems as to date, time, and possible authorship. *Orders for the Two-Thirteen* does appear by itself with the date and location in another collection of poems attributed to Captain T. H. Brown, III; it is also handwritten into Doc Livingood's log and specifically attributed to Theron Hart Brown, III; and, Sandra Brown identified both poems as being written by Theron Hart Brown, III, and contained in the collection of poems in the possession of Theron Brown's relatives.

Tontouta is in New Caledonia and is the location of the airport. It appears in late March 1943 to early April, the squadron left Espiritu Santos and spent time in New Caledonia before returning to Espiritos Santos. Noumea is approximately 40 miles South of Tontouta. Tontouta would also be a stop-over on the way to Australia.

THE BUG OF FATE!

Yes, there's only one way to explain it,
I've decided it really was fate.
For who'd think that a bug brought together,
A cadet and a girl who is great?

I was minding my own damn good business
(It was after my down-check on "B")
When I started to cough and to sniffle,
And a gold-brick decided to be.

Spent two days in the Sick Bay Dispensary,
And I thought I'd be out on the third:
But a pharyngite bug had attacked me-
Left a cough that was really a bird!

"Hmmm – There's only one way to defeat it,"
Said the doc, "So I think we'll send
This young lad to the kind tender mercies
Of the guys up on 'Hospital Bend'".

Now I won't say I'm sorry it happened
For I wasn't up there very long,
When a wise-cracking cute little female
Came into my life like a song.

She was standing right there in the doorway,
(It was easy to see she's a nurse)
And she said, with a pleasant expression,
"Cadet Brown! – Are you better or worse?"

Once recovered from child-like confusion,
And then seeing the chance that I had,
I quick gathered my wits and half muttered,
"I've seen plenty, and, son – that's not bad!!"

So the days that I stayed were a pleasure,
(It was hard, tho', to get magazines)
For she often dropped by isolation

Till I was up and once more on the scenes.

When recovered and back in the running,
I soon gave this sweet girl a few calls;
And we spent many pleasant long hours
At the beach, at shows, and the balls.

There's a moral that goes with this story:-
To be safe as a bachelor mug,
I advise – and it freely is given –
Don't go fooling around with a bug!!!

Guadalcanal – April 11, 1943.
Brown

<u>Comments:</u>   This poem was identified as written by Theron Hart Brown, III, by numerous sources: it was typed on a sheet of paper with "Brown" written at the bottom; it was handwritten into Doc Livingood's log and specifically attributed to Theron Hart Brown, III; it was contained in another collection attributed to Captain T. H. Brown, III; and Sandra Brown identified the poem as being written by Theron and contained in the collection of poems in the possession of Theron Brown's relatives. However, this is the only poem that expressly identifies Theron Brown as the author by an internal reference.

IN MEMORIAM –
WADE H. BRITT, Jr.
Major, USMC,
CO of VMF-213
Ther's no one can take his place
In the hearts of us one and all.
The high and low, the best and worst
Must go when He gives the call.

And now the best of us all is gone –
And it's no disgrace to weep,
But we'll carry on as he taught us to,
While he guides us from his sleep.

Guadalcanal – April 13, 1943.
Brown

<u>Comments:</u>   This poem was identified as written by Theron Hart Brown, III, by numerous sources: it was typed on a sheet of paper with "Brown" written at the bottom; it was contained in another collection attributed to Captain T. H. Brown, III; and Sandra Brown identified the poem as being written by Theron and contained in the collection of poems in the possession of Theron Brown's relatives.

Major Wade H. Britt, Jr., was the Commanding Officer of the VMF-213 and prepared them for combat. Major Britt died on April 13, 1943, in a runway accident. The poem and its authorship as being "Lt. Brown" was identified as being placed on a plaque over his grave on Guadalcanal, also known in code names as Cactus and BVEY.

WHY?

Death Calls!
Some go-
And in going haven't time to pause a
        bit and think
Of the things they leave behind them:
The sun – a woman's kiss – a long and
        cooling drink.

Death calls!
Some stay-
And in staying pause, ponder a bit and
        think;
Then return to the things that are left them:
The sun – woman's kiss – a long and
        cooling drink.

Guadalcanal – April 13, 1943.
Brown

Comments: This poem was identified as written by Theron Hart Brown, III, by numerous sources: it was typed on a sheet of paper with "Brown" written at the bottom; it was contained in another collection attributed to Captain T. H. Brown, III; and Sandra Brown identified the poem as being written by Theron and contained in the collection of poems in the possession of Theron Brown's relatives.

This death-reflective poem is dated the same day as Major Britt's death.

Up There in the Skies

"What do you find up there in the Skies?"
I said.
He smiled to himself; and then lowered
his head.

"There is quiet in the skies.
I know – for I've been there.
There is peace, too;
But not now.

"There is happiness in the skies.
I know – for I've felt it.
There is revenge, too –
In our vow.

"There is beauty in the skies.
I know – for I've seen it.
There is war, too,
And death, now.

"Quiet, peace, happiness, and beauty –
these will last
The many ages through where all hate is past."

Guadalcanal, April 17, 1943.

Comments: While this poem did not have the Brown name typed or written on it, it was included in a smaller collect of poems that were specifically attributed to Captain T. H. Brown, III. Also, Sandra Brown identified the poem as being written by Theron and contained in the collection of poems in the possession of Theron Brown's relatives. Additionally, none of the copies had a title. The title used herein was taken from the poem's first line.

"SNA FU"

In the Navy it's proper, and quite alright
And considered the thing to do,
To abbreviate each thing you write
To save a line or two.

There's the ComNoumea and the ComSoPac
And the BuNavPersonnel,
And, oh – don't forget the boss of the pack,
The one called Cominch as well.

OpNav and BuAero, and the ComPacFleet,
And the ComTaskFor number Two.
But the one that's got the whole lot beat
Is the unofficial SNAFU.

With a dignified stance and respectful poise,
Without a grin on your kisser,
Just ask a question of one of the Boys –
You cannot fail to miss 'er.

"No the time's not right, and the stuff's not here;
And the Admiral's feeling blue.
It's out of the question, old man, this year."
There, mister, you've met SNAFU.

When your squadron moves to a far-flung base,
And they say with a frown, "Who're you?
We didn't expect you. Dump any place!"
There again, my lad, SNAFU!

You're waiting in "Dago" in ARS;
You're mustering three times a day.
You don't fly – you just sit and wait;
Lord, yes!
SNAFU! – and it's here to stay.

Yes, the Situation's normal – All Fouled Up,
And it certainly is a shame.

But you learn it young, when you're just a pup.
It's part of the Navy game!!

Guadalcanal – April 20, 1943.

<u>Comments:</u> While this poem did not have the "Brown" name typed or written on it, it was included in a smaller collect of poems that were specifically attributed to Captain T. H. Brown, III. Also, Sandra Brown identified the poem as being written by Theron and contained in the collection of poems in the possession of Theron Brown's relatives.

IN FLIGHT

In flight I seek and find fair Heaven's prize,
As free of care I skim the earth below,
And speeding, darting, playing learn to know
The freedom God created in the skies.
Scenes only Heaven yields can thrill these eyes
Which from on high have seen the sunset's glow,
The birth of stars and planets row on row,
And beauties God to earth-bound man denies.
For I have lived with birds and clouds and stars,
And shared the secrets known to air-borne things;
And soared far beyond the hold of man-made bars,
And felt vast power surging through my wings.
In flying I have transcended man's estate,
And found through space a path to Heaven's Gate.

A Sonnet
Guadalcanal – May 7, 1943.

Comments: While this poem did not have the Brown name typed or written on it, it was included in a smaller collect of poems that were specifically attributed to Captain T. H. Brown, III. Also, that copy, although missing the words, "A Sonnet" and Guadalcanal – May 7, 1947" was annotated with the following:
    "Written by Capt. T. H. Brown, III, U.S.M.C.R.
    Summer of 1943. Somewhere in the So. Pacific."

Additionally, Sandra Brown identified the poem as being written by Theron and contained in the collection of poems in the possession of Theron Brown's relatives.

Letter To:

Dear Mother, Father, Sister, Wife, and Friend
Of that fine boy who flew away to die,
Who fought for right and freedom in the sky,
And fighting, prove his worth – and met his end;
I write this message Billy asked I send.
The bravery of his words and feeling my
Poor efforts can't convey; but still I'll try.
"If I should go, this favor you can lend,"
He said, "Please tell them life was not in vain,
For all it's riches it has showered on me.
I've worked and played; I've loved, was loved. The pain
Death leaves with them my one regret will be.
They've made my life complete, though short its span."
He died for his belief. He died a man.

A Sonnet
Guadalcanal – June 24, 1943.
 Brown

<u>Comment:</u>   This poem was identified as written by Theron Hart Brown, III, by numerous sources: it was typed on a sheet of paper with "Brown" written at the bottom; it was contained in another collection attributed to Captain T. H. Brown, III; and Sandra Brown, the wife of Theron's brother, Sherwood P. Brown, identified the poem as being written by Theron and contained in the collection of poems in the possession of Theron Brown's relatives.

The Plane In Flight

A silhouette against the distant sky,
The sun's reflection gleaming off a wing,
A moment's flash, a shining man-made thing,
This is the plane in flight.

A flickering shadow speeding past a cloud,
A silver spectre mirrored by the sun,
The great ambition of the ages won:
This is the plane in flight.

The roaring song of sturdy strength and pow'r
A song of motion, liquid, swift, and pure,
Which sings an answer to this heav'n borne lure:
This is the plane in flight.

There are no words, no phrases knit to toll
The story of the pain – of man's travail
To mold this dream. It tells its own great tale:
This is the plain in flight.

Espiritu Santo – August 1, 1943.

<u>Comments:</u>   This poem was identified as written by Theron Hart Brown, III, by numerous sources: it was typed on a sheet of paper with "Brown" written at the bottom; it was contained in another collection attributed to Captain T. H. Brown, III; and Sandra Brown, the wife of Theron's brother, Sherwood P. Brown, identified the poem as being written by Theron and contained in the collection of poems in the possession of Theron Brown's relatives.

Dedication to Major Weissenberger upon the event of his transfer out of the squadron:

They've taken our leader away from us,
He's now got a desk – a boy's job
Ace Greg's too busy to fight any more;
He's clothing the naked mob.

Oh, woe is me! Alas and alack!
He'll fight no more in this war.
It's scivvies and socks and Khaki pants,
And "How are things down at the store?"

But kidding aside – and all that stuff,
We'll miss "Slim Jim" you know.
A damn good leader, a damn good scout;
We hated to see him go.

He took the place of a man we loved,
And he did it mighty well.
He talked for us and he fought for us,
And he led us through all the hell.

Now back we go, and It's "So long Greg!"
And "we hope you'll like G-4!"
Remember us from behind that desk
As we're rolling up the score.

Espiritu Santo – September 1, 1943
Brown

<u>Comments:</u>   This poem was identified as written by Theron Hart Brown, III, by numerous sources: it was typed on a sheet of paper with "Brown" written at the bottom; it was contained in another collection attributed to Captain T. H. Brown, III; and Sandra Brown identified the poem as being written by Theron and contained in the collection of poems in the possession of Theron Brown's relatives. The identical version of this poem in the other collection of poems had a more elaborate dedication and was signed by twelve members of the squadron.

The formal dedication preceding the poem read:

Marine Fighter Squadron
Two Thirteen

In consideration of his qualities of leadership and
personality which have endeared him to us. This tribute is of-
fered to Major Gregory Weissenberger by the undersign-
ed members of the original combat team of VMF-213. We
wish to express our gratitude of having had the privilege
of serving under him and fighting beside him. The follow-
ing poem, such as it is, is dedicated to him, and presented
to him at the time of his transfer from his squadron to other
duties. We bow to the good of the service, but with mingled
pride and regret that the gain to group eleven must be balanc-
ed by the corresponding loss to Marine Fighting Squadron
Two Thirteen.

The poem was signed by:

Ted Brown
Milt Vedder
W.J. (Gus) Thomas
Wally Cloake
J. L. Morgan, Jr.
Edward O. Shaw
James N. Cupp
A. R. Boag
Bill Livingood
Sterling M. Harrison
George C. DeFabio
L. W. McCleary

OVER THE HORIZON

There's a story that needs telling
Of our friends that don't come back
Of the boys who've left our Hell Hawks
Of the comrades that we lack.

There was Britt and Tate and Eckart,
There was Peck and Poncho too.
Every one of them is gone now,
But their mem'ries follow through.

When the legends that will follow
Are all spun in years to come,
We will talk of these dead heros,
They who died to sink the Sun.

Was there ever squadron so gifted
As were we with Britt to lead?
Was there ever a squadron struck harder
By a more ill-fated dead?

A man loved as well as respected
From the low to high in ranks
To have known and followed this leader
Was an honor. We give our thanks.

Then of Tate we'll all remember
How he grinned and laughed away
All the luck misfortune sent him
Up until that fateful day.

And of Eckart, unassuming
With his pipe and quiet way
Of the four who turned back forty
Its' for Lee we stopped to pray.

Next of those whose names we honor
Was a boy in years and ken,
But he flew and fought a veteran;

Peck was liked by all his men.

There is naught but good to say now
Of the one shot down in flame.
All the oldest of the Hell Hawks
Will long honor Poncho's name.

That's the story needed telling
Of our friends who won't come back.
There are others who are missing,
Other comrades that we lack.

There is Winnia and Spoede,
There is "Bluebeard" Votaw, too.
There's a chance they'll be returning
And we fondly pray they do.

Tho' we've gotten 67,
And we've only lost these 8
And these 8 are all we've lost
We'd return the 67,
For not one is worth the cost.

Brown

<u>Comments:</u>   In addition to the handwritten name of Brown on the original and its inclusion in the other collection of poems attributed to Captain T. H. Brown, III, this poem seems to chronologically fit the authorship of Theron Brown, who was killed in action on September 12, 1943. The poem chronicles the deaths of VMF-213 members and those missing in action (MIA) but predates Captain Brown's death. Sandra Brown specifically identified this poem as one in her collection that had the notation, South Pacific Summer 1943. The pilots mentioned in the poem are:

"Britt" -   Wade H. Britt, Died
Tate -   Don H. Tate
Eckart -   Leland L. Eckart
Pec -   Milton E. Peck
Poncho -   Foy R. Garison
Winnia -   Charles C. Winnia
Spoede -   Herman H. Spoede
"Bluebeard" Votaw -   R. W. Votaw

Section B – Poems Identified with WWII Marines in the South Pacific

THE GRAVES OF GAVUTU

They rise from the graves of Gavutu,
These ghosts of the shattered dead,
And they walk on the shores of Gavutu
With a bewildered, aimless tread.

They rise from the graves of Gavutu,
These souls of American men,
Who died on the shores of Gavutu
That others might live again.

They rise from the graves of Gavutu,
And face a western land,
And words the west wind carries
They do not understand.

For the wind brings word of bickering
And of the state of "civilian morale,"
While here on the shores of Gavutu
They died in a living hell.

And here on the shores of Gavutu
The ghost of a private speaks well,
"What do they mean, sarge," he asks,
"When they talk of "civilian morale?"

Sgt. Frank W. McCulloch

<u>Comments:</u>   This poem appears only in Doc Livingood's records on a separately typed sheet. The author Frank McCulloch enlisted in the U.S. Marine Corps in 1942 but a medical condition kept him stateside. Frank McCulloch spent the war writing up the heroic deeds of Marines for the Marines' public information office in San Francisco. After the war, McCulloch returned to Reno to write for the Reno Evening Gazette, where he got his first taste of investigative reporting. He had a long and distinguished career as an investigative reporter. On May 3, 2011, Frank McCulloch confirmed he had written the poem, *The Graves of Gavutu*. The Poem was published in Leatherneck magazine in February 1943.

The battle for Gavutu and Tanambogo, occurred in August of 1942. Joined by a narrow causeway, these two small spots of land had been developed before the war as a Royal Australian Air Force seaplane base. After the Japanese took the Southern Solomons in early May 1942, they continued that use, and had over five hundred to one thousand men stationed on these islands. There were several four-engine patrol seaplanes and single-engine floatplane fighters when dawn broke on August 7; these aircraft were destroyed by U.S. carrier planes. The Japanese occupants of the islands, a mixture of aviation personnel, construction troops and Special Naval Landing Force "marines," defended the islands.

The Photographs below are from the Department of the Navy, Naval Historical Center.

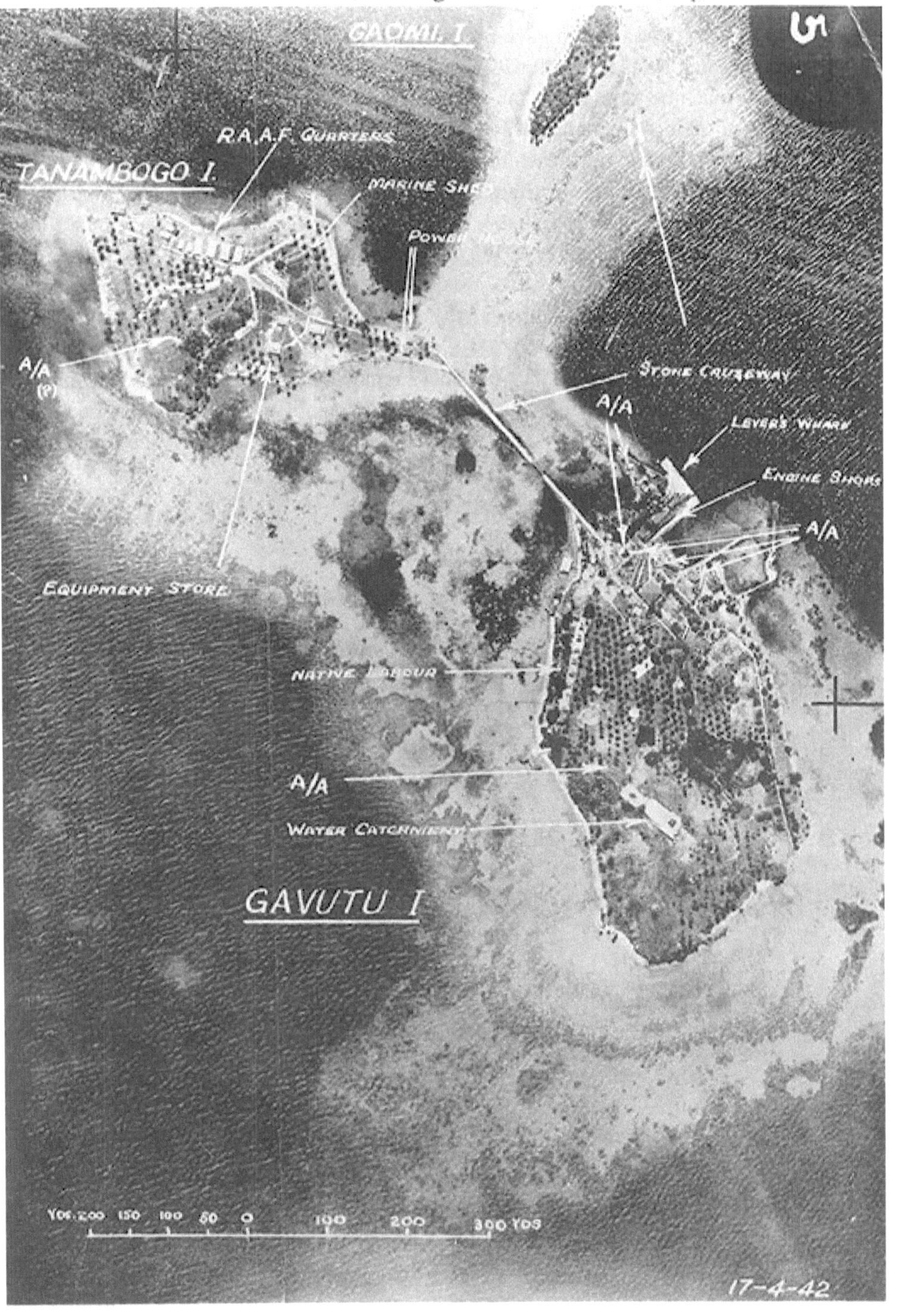
GAOMI I.
TANAMBOGO I.
R.A.A.F. QUARTERS
MARINE SHED
POWER HOUSE
STONE CAUSEWAY
LEVER'S WHARF
ENGINE SHOPS
A/A
A/A
A/A
(P)
EQUIPMENT STORE
NATIVE LABOUR
A/A
WATER CATCHMENT
GAVUTU I
YDS 200 150 100 50 0 100 200 300 YDS
17-4-42

Gavutu and Tanambogo gave the Japanese good defensive positions. Each island was dominated by a large hill, while buildings and entrenchments provided cover for Japanese machine guns and small artillery pieces. A brief pre-landing bombardment did little to reduce the defenses, so casualties were serious when U.S. Marines came ashore on Gavutu's northeastern side at about noon on August 7th. Fighting continued on that island for the rest of the day, through the night and into August 8th before Gavutu was reasonably secure. Meanwhile, Marine reserves had been called over from Guadalcanal to Tulagi and Gavutu-Tanambogo.

A small Marine attack on Tanambogo had failed during the evening of the August 7th. In the morning, fresh Marines reinforcements arrived on Gavutu. After a heavy bombardment by

U. S. Navy ships, landings began on Tanambogo, and by nightfall the island was basically in American hands. The cost of taking Gavutu and Tanambogo was seventy Marine lives; there were few Japanese survivors.

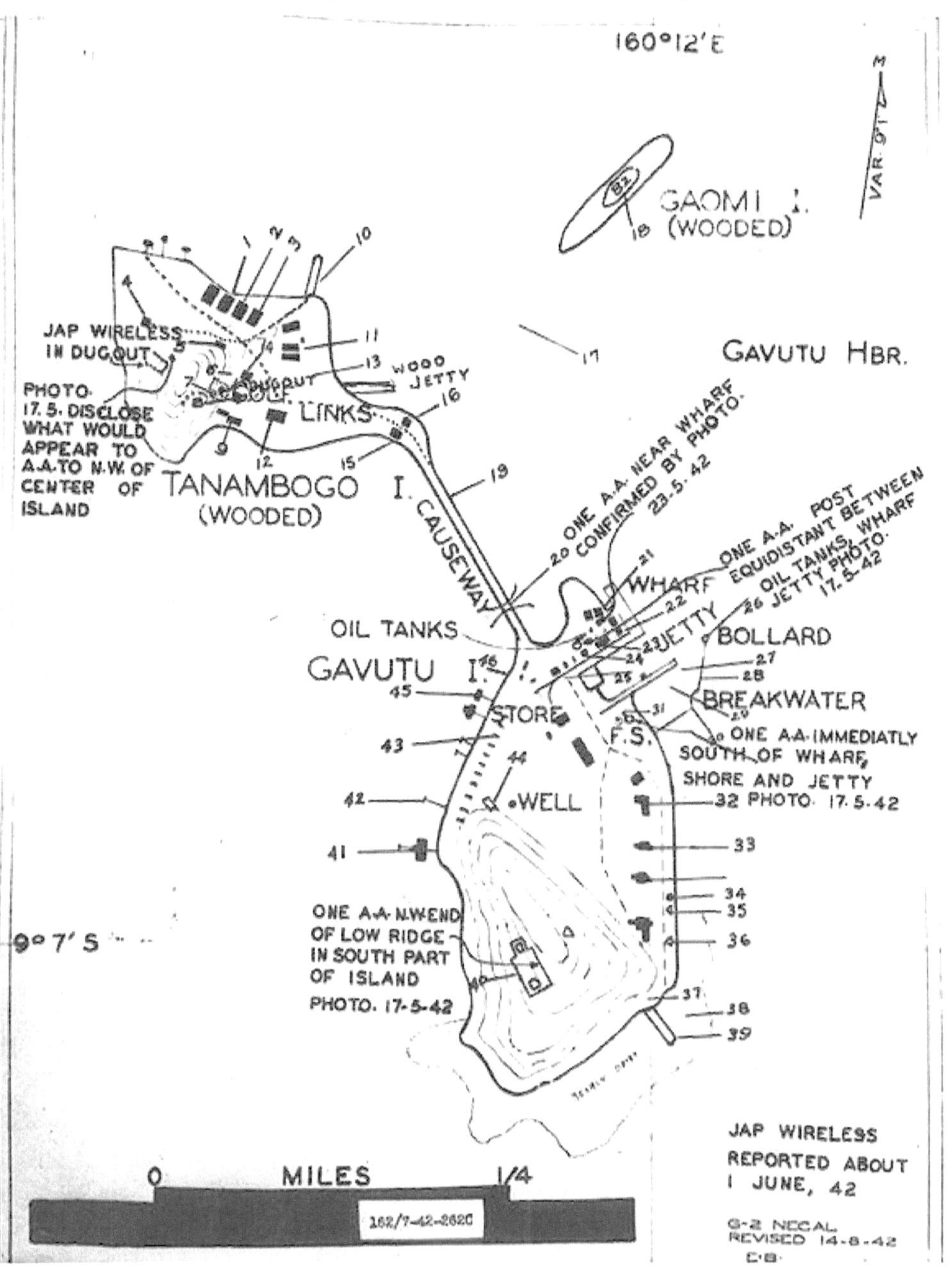
160°12'E
VAR. 9°12'E
GAOMI I.
(WOODED)
GAVUTU HBR.
JAP WIRELESS
IN DUGOUT
PHOTO.
17.5. DISCLOSE
WHAT WOULD
APPEAR TO
A.A. TO N.W. OF
CENTER OF
ISLAND
GOLF
LINKS
DUGOUT
WOOD
JETTY
TANAMBOGO
(WOODED)
I. CAUSEWAY
ONE A.A. NEAR WHARF
CONFIRMED BY PHOTO.
23.5.42
ONE A.A. POST
EQUIDISTANT BETWEEN
OIL TANKS, WHARF
JETTY PHOTO.
17.5.42
OIL TANKS
WHARF
JETTY
BOLLARD
GAVUTU I.
STORE
BREAKWATER
F.S.
ONE A.A. IMMEDIATLY
SOUTH OF WHARF,
SHORE AND JETTY
PHOTO. 17.5.42
WELL
ONE A.A. N.W. END
OF LOW RIDGE
IN SOUTH PART
OF ISLAND
PHOTO. 17-5-42
9°7'S
0   MILES   1/4
JAP WIRELESS
REPORTED ABOUT
I JUNE, 42
G-2 NECAL.
REVISED 14-8-42
C.B.

Key to the numbered features on Photo #NH 97748:

1. Store Hut
2. & 3. Army Huts
4. Bomb Store Hut
5. 2nd Fuel Store
6. Rails (wooden)
7. Fuel oil stores
8. Kitchen
9. Wash House
10. Wharf, depth 15'
11. Repair for riggers and a few stores
12. Officers mess and late headquarters for VNTG RAAF wireless
13. Golf course
14. Ratings quarters
15. Engine house
16. Power House
17. Cable (no- connection)
18. Gaomi Island (Dead Mans Island)
19. Causeway
20. Bridge 20' length
21. Gunpit
22. Elevated concrete span
23. & 24. Stores
25. Boat shed
26. Bollard
27. Wire fence
28. Break water
29. Swimming pool
30. Gunpit
31. Levers Bros. Office
32. Bachelor's quarters
33. Accountants house
34. Gunpit
35. & 36. Wireless tripod masts
37. & 38. Small square entrenchments
39. Wharf not in use
40. Water catchment
41. The unused house

42. Latrines

43. Native quarters

44. (left blank on original list)

45. Chinese quarters

46. *Store*

"OUR FIGHTING MEN"

A marine told his buddies on Guadalcanal,
"The Army is coming, think of it, pal!"
His corp. answered him "Alright then–
Let's build a nice clubhouse for Our Fighting Men.

They can have entertainments and may-be a play,
Recreation advisors from W.P.A.,
USO hostesses, and movies galore,
For the Army gives morale a very high score."

"One thing," said the chow hound, "We'll eat better now.
Depend on the Army to drag in the chow.
They'll start post-exchanges, have ice cream no end.
Life has to be pleasant for Our Fighting Men."

A Sea-bea rolled up and asked "What's the score,
The cruisers and wagons all laying off-shore,
While scads of destroyers are sweeping the bay?
Is the Army finally landing today?"

They dashed up the beach when the boats hit the sand,
Steel helmets, fixed bayonets and rifles in hand.
Marines washing clothes asked, "You lads going far?
What the hell is your hurry? Have you heard of a war?"

"Shut up!" said the Sgt., "Go limber your legs;
And trade this Jap helmet for a case of real eggs.
This barking at soldiers must come to an end.
You must be respectful toward Our Fighting Men."

Their Generals outrank ours, so they'll take command.
New rules and new orders will govern the land.
They'll have some MP's to show us around,
When the Army takes over, it sure shakes the ground.

"We can take it", said the Raider, "It won't be long
Before the Admiral bellers, and we'll shove on.
And a little while later we'll be landing again,

To make Bougainville safe for Our Fighting Men.

Guadalcanal – January, 1943.

<u>Comment:</u>   The date on this poem predates the deployment of the VMF-213 and was not included in the smaller group of poems attributed to Captain T. H. Brown, III.   Additionally, in Sandra Brown's collection, it was indicated as Anonymous.

However, the poem was published in the Marine Corp Gazette on December 1943 in an article written by Lieutenant General Thomas Holomb, U.S. Marine Corp. The poem was referenced as being authored by "one of our men" – basically anonymous. The article was derived from a speech given in a Navy Day address delivered at the Navy League dinner in New York, October 27, 1943.

THE ROAD TO GIZO BAY

By the old Guadalcanal pagoda,
Where the needle passes free,
They've cooked up a hot assignment
for Marine Group 23.
As the wind howls thru the palm trees,
you hear Operations say,
Load the belly tanks with juice boys,
take the scouts to Gizo Bay.

Chorus:

Hit the road to Gizo Bay,
Where the Jap fleet spends the day,
You can hear the duds a-chunkin'
from Rabaul to Lunga Bay.
Pack a load to Gizo Bay,
Where the float plane Zeros play,
And the bombs come down like thunder
on the natives 'cross the way.

                    2.
Take me somewhere East of Ewa,
Where the best ain't like the worst;
Where there ain't no Doug MacArthur,
And a man can drown of thirst.
For the Army takes the medals,
and the Navy takes the queens,
But the boys that take the
rooking is the United States Marines.

Lt. Hindricks – Mag-23.

<u>Comments:</u>   This poem/song only appears in Doc Livingood's collection. The
poem was written in the time period that Theron Brown would have been able to
author the poem with first-hand accounts of its content. "Lt. Hindricks – Mag-23"

appearing after the poem/Song suggests the author and no further information is available.

Evidently, the marines and soldiers often sung such ditties on Guadalcanal. Several versions can be found on the internet and one in the book <u>The Battle for Guadalcanal</u>, by Samuel Griffith. This particular ditty was sung to the tune of "On the Road to Mandalay." The Poem/Song in Doc Livingood's collection seems to be the most complete.

MAG-23, Marine Air Group-23, was commissioned at Ewa, Territory of Hawaii, as part of the Second Marine Aircraft Wing; the group became the first Marine aviation group to meet the enemy in the South Pacific. The group formed the forward echelon of the First Marine Aircraft Wing and landed its first units at Henderson Field on 20 August 1942. MAG-23, augmented by Army and Navy land based air under the operational control of 1st MAW, furnished air support to the First Marine Division and Army ground forces in the Solomon Islands campaign.

In the Summer of 1943, the campaign advance northward in the Solomons to the New Georgia group of islands. Landings on New Georgia began as early as June 1943.

Gizo is a city with a harbor situated on the island of Ghizo (different spelling, same pronunciation) in the New Georgia Islands. The Island is often referred to as Gizo in World War II documents. During the Japanese occupation of Guadalcanal, Gizo was a Japanese barge repair facility and way station that the Japanese used to reinforce their garrison on Guadalcanal. After the United States took Guadalcanal, the Japanese used these bases for attacks on Guadalcanal.

It was just off Ghizo where John F. Kennedy gained fame after his Patrol Boat PT109 was rammed by a Japanese destroyer. At nearby Plum Pudding Island (often called Kennedy Island), John F. Kennedy swam ashore.

Rabaul, on the eastern portion of New Guinea, was the capital East New Britain and is spread around the rim of Simpson Harbor, Rabaul was the main base in the Japanese Southeast Area and was well situated to support Japanese advances southward and in their defense as the Allied forces moved north in the Solomons. The Solomon campaign was initiated to capture Rabaul. Currently, East New Britain is a province of Papua New Guinea.

WHAT MAKES A MARINE

It isn't his set of 'Blues',
Or his mirror-shined shoes,
Or his uniform of greens,
That makes a Marine.

It isn't how he can drink,
Or how often he's been in the clink,
Or how many lands he's seen,
That makes a Marine.

A Leatherneck is more than that;
More than a medal or a campaign hat –
More than a hashmark or a couple of stripes,
Or idle scuttlebutt or perpetual gripes,
This is but a cloak – the dress Marine.
Not the naked truth which the enemy's seen.
Ask the enemy what a Leatherneck is.
The enemy will tell you this:
It's his meeting a foe of superior might.
Unmindful of numbers and ready to fight;
It's a landing, a spearhead, a challenge, a raid
With bullet and bayonet, knife and grenade;
It's his stamina, sacrifice, courage, his 'guts'
In obeying an order with no 'if's or buts'
It's his living in foxholes, in muck and mud,
Resisting defeat to his last drop of blood;
It's his tightening his belt when rations are low,
And his open-eyed slumber lest muster should blow,
It's his feverish thirst when the "Lyster bag's" shot,
And his foul-smelling filth when water is not;
It's his conquest of darkness and barbed-wire fence
And dodging the shrapnel with breathless suspense;
It's his dodging thru Hell to find Victory.
And at last he watches the enemy flee
And the Red, White, & Blue waves "tis well" o'ver the scene,
It's the lump in his throat that makes a Marine.

<u>Comment:</u>   This poem was printed on a sheet of paper with no indication of authorship, but it was included in a smaller group of poems specifically attributed to Captain T. H. Brown, III. However, in Sandra Brown's Collection, the poem was indicated as Anonymous.

The "lyster bag" is primarily a dispensing unit for purified or distilled water. These bags are sturdy, watertight, and readily collapsible for packing. Water is withdrawn through small faucets at the bottom. When no other purification equipment is available, the lyster bag can be used to disinfect raw water.

Expressions of a Marine's opinion concerning the organization of the Navy, Army, & the Marine Corps into one body:

Aye, politicians, send us out,
To fight our country's war,
And while we're raising hell out here
Disband our gallant corps.

Just tear the globe and anchor down,
Cut out the eagle's heart,
Clad all of us in olive drab,
And split us far apart;

Take out the two-tone suits of blue,
Reclaim our threadbare "Greens",
But these traditions still belong
To the United States Marines.

Belleau Woods, Chateau Thierry,
St. Mihiel, The Argonne,
Wake Island, Midway The Solomons,
Where have these memories gone?

"Tis better far to take our band
And group us all alone,
(You'll have to search the far flung fronts,
You won't find us at home).

Then give us all the guns we need
With cartridges to spare,
And send us to Japan itself
To make a landing there.

Beneath the cannons thunderous roar
On hot and bloody sands,
While "Wildcats" strafe from up above
Let the Leathernecks make their stand.

When the "Devil-dog" insignia

Waves over Nippon's shores,
Then let the Gods of war decide
The disbandment of our Corps.

<u>Comments:</u>   While the copy of this poem had no indication of authorship, it was included in a group of poems specifically attributed to Captain T. H. Brown, III. However, in Sandra Brown's collection, this poem was indicated as Anonymous.

EDSON'S RIDGE

".....who's there!" – a shot! machine guns stuttered .....
That's just the way it started,
That holocaust of blood and flame,
Where weary pals were parted.

"They're down below and on our flanks!"
This word was passed about,
When suddenly from on our left,
There came this awful shout –

"They've fixed their steel and here they come,
A runnin' and a screamin'!
Hold your ground an' give 'em hell,
And cut them till they're streamin' ..... "

Three times they came and thrice they fell,
Bewildered-, beaten -, broken;
And then they knew, and knew it well -,
That Edson's men weren't jokin'!

Many were the men we lost,
That bloody hellish night;
But through that blood and hell WE FOUGHT
And fought with all our might.

Then came the silence of the dawn,
The dawn that we had prayed for.
The battle's won! – And rest is here;
The rest that we made way for.

The Japs, I doubt, will ne'er forget
That night they tried to raid us.
When asked who beat them at their game,
They'll utter, "Edson's Raiders!"

Pvt. James G. Hall

<u>Comments:</u>   This poem is found in Doc Livingood's collection and no other

collections; however, the poem was published in a Marine magazine, Leatherneck, in March 1943 and authored by Private James G. Hall with a notation after his name, "An Edson Raider."

The bloody battle of Edson's Ridge occurred in September 1942 after the marines landed on Guadalcanal and secured Henderson Field.   The ridge overlooked Henderson field. The Marine commanders noted the same hilltop and arranged to defend it with Marines, already bloodied by actions on Gavutu and Tulagi.

The Japanese probed the Marine positions heavily on the September 12th and attacked on the night of September 13th.

James G. Hall was presented with the Silver Star:

> "The President of the United States of America takes pleasure
> in presenting the Silver Star to Private James G. Hall (MCSN:
> 351522), United States Marine Corps Reserve, for conspicuous
> gallantry and intrepidity while serving with the First Marine
> Raider Battalion in action against Japanese forces in the Solomon
> Islands Area on 7 August 1942. Undeterred by a devastating
> barrage of hostile machine gun and sniper fire from concealed
> positions in cliff commanding the shore line, Private Hall
> unhesitatingly risked his life to rescue his platoon leader who was
> lying wounded in an exposed position. Although a comrade had
> been killed in one of two prior unsuccessful rescue attempts,
> Private Hall worked his way forward under a hail of enemy fire and
> reaching the platoon leader only to find that he was dead from the
> burst of a second hostile shell, move the body to safety. By his
> courage and unselfish efforts in behalf of another at great risk to
> his own life, Private Hall upheld the highest traditions of the
> United States Naval Service."

THE U. S. MARINES

Where they see the "Globe and Anchor"
On your hat or service cap –
They're bound to recognize in you
A patriotic chap:
A lad who heard his country's call
When danger threatened nigh –
A leatherneck who volunteered
To keep "Old Glory" high.

You're a member of a legion
That holds God and Freedom dear –
The pride of all America
A valiant volunteer:
You're a credit to your Nation
And the Corps feels mighty proud
To know the "Globe and Anchor"
Makes you stand out in a crowd.

Sgt. Timothy J. Riley

<u>Comments:</u>   This poem was found in Doc Livingood's collection and in no other collection; however, the poem was published in the Marine Corp magazine, Leatherneck, in February 1943. The poem was authored by Sgt. Timothy J. Riley.

THE ONLY WAY TO WIN

It takes a little courage,
And a little self-control,
And some grim determination,
If you want to reach a goal.

It takes a deal of striving,
And a firm and stern set chin,
No matter what the battle,
If your really out to win.

There's no easy road to glory,
There's no rosy road to fame,
Life, however we may view it,
Is no simple parlor game.

But it's prizes call for fighting,
For endurance and fore gut,
For a rugged disposition
And a "don't know when to quit".

Comments: While this poem had no identifying features in Doc. Livingood's collection, it was in the smaller collection of poems attributed to Captain T. H. Brown, III. In Sandra Brown's collection the poem was indicated as Anonymous but with the additional comment, "possibly by Capt. Brown."

Song of the Island

On Guadalcanal you better park
When the light fades out in the tropic dark,
Or you'll hear the song of the Cactus nights,
"Hey you! Turn out them _ _ _ _ _ _ _ lights!"

Condition red or condition green,
Just strike a match in the tropic scene
To hear the chorus of Cactus nights,
 "Hey you! Turn out them _ _ _ _ _ _ _ lights!"

Colonel, General, Seargeant (sic) Major,
Light a lamp and it's a wager,
You'll hear the song of Cactus nights,
 "Hey you! Turn out them _ _ _ _ _ _ _ lights!"

And you better turn out them _ _ _ _ _ _ _ lights
When you hear the song of Cactus nights.
A Marine is looking down his sights,
And he'll shoot as one of his sacred rights,
If you don't turn out them _ _ _ _ _ _ _ lights.

<u>Comments:</u>   This poem was found only in Doc Livingood's Flight Surgeon's log, page 139. It was handwritten and anonymous.
   Cactus was a code name for Guadalcanal.

A Poem Fresh from Australia

A perfect face is hard to find,
But harder still is a neat behind.
Some far too thin - some much to plump,
Yet others with unsightly bumps.
Some closely cased their contours hide,
Some gaily gig from side to side.
And some that wobble – blithe and gay –
Bulge badly in the oddest way!
Some near the shoulder blades are found,
Whilst others barely clear the ground;
And some delight the artists' eye
While some, it seems, don't even try.
The perfect face it seems to me,
(If you're observant, you'll agree)
That makes the hardened heart go thump,
So seldom tops the perfect rump.

<u>Comments:</u>   This poem was found only in Doc Livingood's Flight Surgeon's log,
page 140.
It was handwritten and anonymous.

Ode to the End of Time

In the deep Pacific so far away
The Lord must have lost his temper one day
And in his wrath he thumbed his nose,
And on that spot an island rose.

A Hell on earth, believe me, Pal!
This miserable place became –
A place where every man is weaned
On bright yellow pills called Atabrine!

Where a torrid sun burns flaming red
And makes a man wish he were dead,
A spot where a man draws his lot
Of fever and jaundice and tropical rot.

Where every man is sure to wear
A nest of ants in his hair,
For freedom's sake we came to fight,
For people's sake we fought with might.

For justices sake we made Tojo run.
For our soldiers sake the fight was won,
For our country's sake we were willing to roam,
But now for Christ's sake, let's go home.

Albin J. Pearson
33 C.B.

<u>Comments:</u>   This poem was handwritten into Doc Livingood's Flight Surgeon Journal on page 141 and appears attributed to Albin J. Pearson; however, no information could be found on Albin Pearson. The letters C.B. often applies to the Navy Construction Battalions, better known as Seabees.

Early in the war a campaign, in the prevention of malaria, a synthetic drug, sold under the name of Atabrine and invented by a German researcher before the war, was distributed to American troops stationed on the South Pacific islands. Complaints against the yellow pills became common. Atabrine was bitter, appeared to impart its own sickly hue to the skin. Some of its side effects were headaches, nausea, and vomiting, and in a few cases it produced a temporary psychosis. Two

VMF-213 pilots, Hall and Thomas, were recorded as having reaction to atabrine, page 61 of the Flight Surgeon's Log.

Tojo Hideki, (1884-1948), was a Japanese political and military leader and the premier who ordered the attack on Pearl Harbor in 1941.

Tropical Duty

A Marine in a corner, quiet and glum
Stripped to the waist and burned by the sun
Crouched by a box with a candle's faint flame
With inspiration he dare not name
He wrote these words to the rhythm of the rain.

Where there aint no ten commandments
And a man can raise a thirst
We're the outcasts of civilization
The victims of life at its worst.

Down in the rain soaked islands
Are the men that God forgot
Battling the treacherous fever
The itch and tropical rot.

Now nobody knows they are living
And nobody gives a damn
Back home they are soon forgotten
These Marines of Uncle Sam.

Marines on "Foreign Duty"
Earning their meager pay
Guarding the country's millions
On a dot of land so far away.

Living with dirty natives
Down in the sweltering zone
Dreaming of wines and loved ones
Eight thousand miles from home.

Drenched with sweat in the evening
They sit on their bunks and dream
Killing themselves with Gook beer
To drown memory's horrible to dream.

Vermin at night on your pillow
Its that, no doctor can cure

Hell, they're not convicts
Just Marines on a "foreign tour."

<u>Comments:</u>   This poem was only found handwritten in Doc Livingood's Flight Surgeon log on page 142 & 143 and was anonymous.

Map Appendices

1. Pilot's Reference Strip (Front and Back) – Solomon Islands
2. Vila and Munda Point Airdromes - New Georgia Group
3. Kahili and Ballale Airdomes – Bougainvile Island.
4. Buka Passage Airdrome – Buka Island.

The maps on the next page are on a Pilot's Reference Strip Map of the Solomon Islands; both the front and back are shown. The three maps on the back of the strip are enlarged on the following three pages.

Markings occur on Kolombangara Island close to "Villa Airdrome" and on New Georgia Island at the Munda Point Airdrome, map 2, on Bougainville Island at the Kahili Airdrome and on Ballale Island Airdrome, map 3, and on Buka Island at the Buka Passage Airdrome, map 4. These markings appear to have been added for further identification.

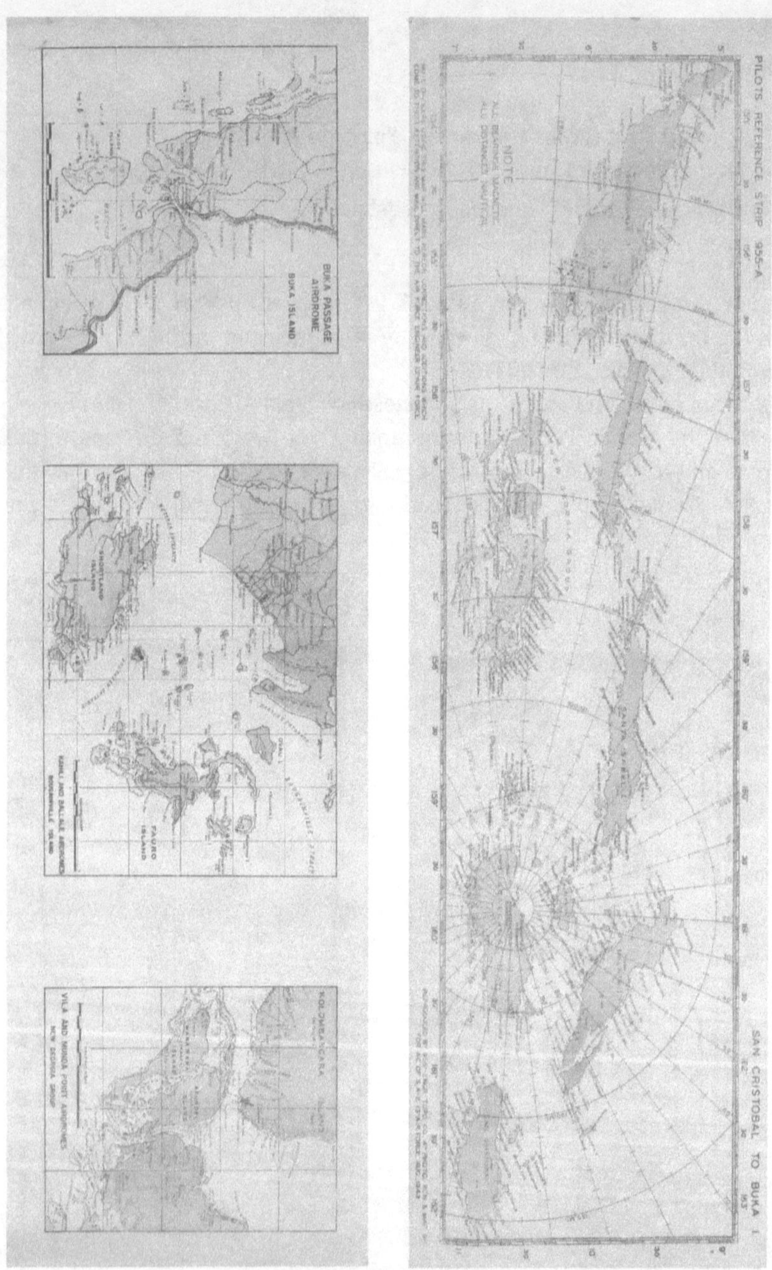

1. **Pilot's Reference Strip MAP (Front and Back) – Solomon Islands appears on the following.**

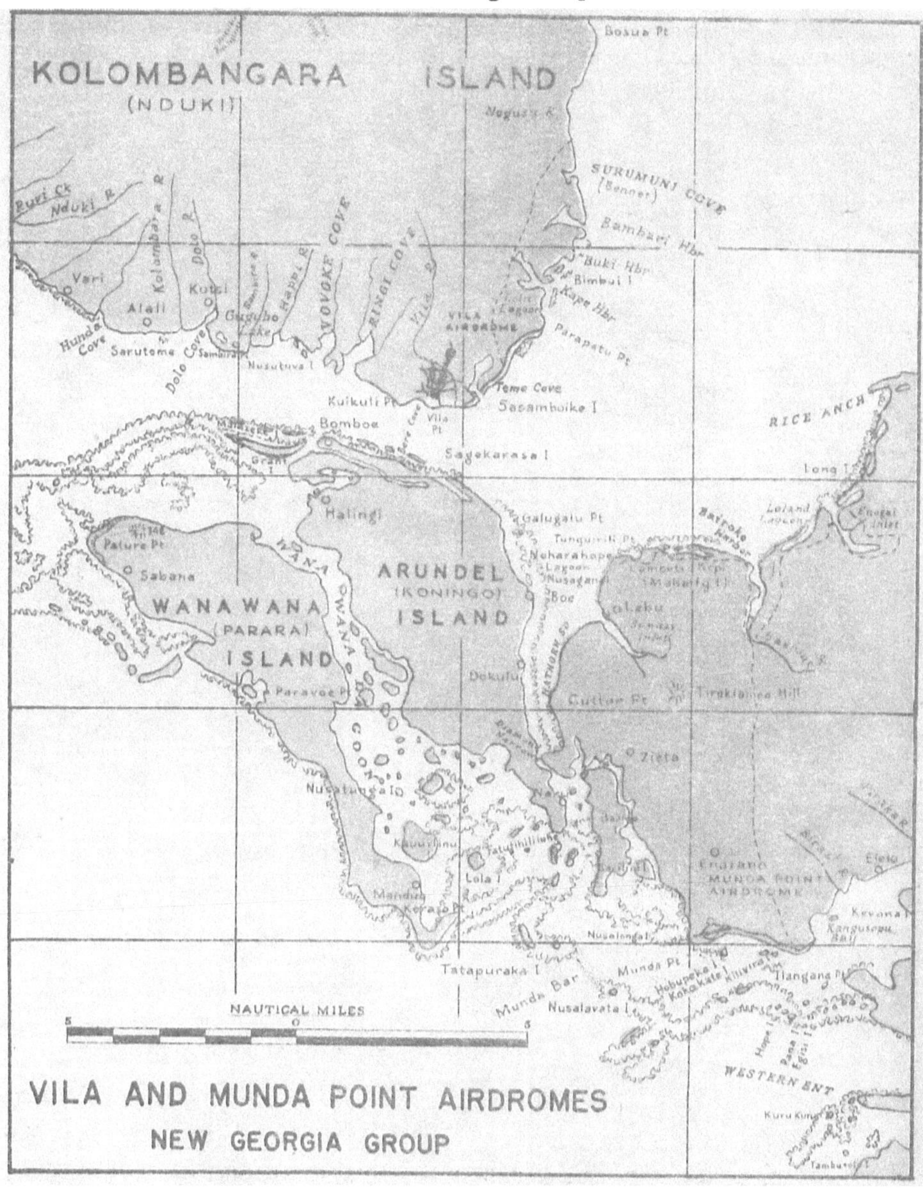

KOLOMBANGARA   ISLAND
(NDUKI)
Bosua Pt
Noguzu R.
SURUMUNI COVE
(Sonner)
Bambari Hbr
Buri Ck
Nduki R.
Kolombara R.
Dolo R.
Hapa R.
VOVOKE COVE
RINGI COVE
Vila
Buki Hbr
Bimbul I.
Kopo Hbr
Vari
Kutai
VILA AIRDROME
VILA Lagoon
Parapatu Pt
Alali
Gogoho Lake
Hunda Cove
Sarutome
Dolo Cove
Sambara
Nusutuva I.
Teme Cove
Sasamboike I.
Kuikuli Pt
Vila Pt
RICE ANCH
Bomboe
Sagekarasa I.
Long I.
Grant
Halingi
Galugalu Pt
Loland Lagoon
Enogai Inlet
Palure Pt
Tunguru Pt
Neharahope
Bairoko Harbor
Sabana
Lagoon
Nusagan
Boe
Lumbari Kop
(Makuti I.)
WANAWANA
(PARARA)
ISLAND
WANAWANA LAGOON
ARUNDEL
(KONINGO)
ISLAND
Oleku
Diamond Narrows
Tirokiamea Hill
BATHORN RIVER
Paravae I.
Dekulu
Cutter Pt
Zieta
Nusatupa ID.
Naro
Kauvilinu
Tatuthilliuhi
Enavano
MUNDA POINT
AIRDROME
Kevana
Kangusupu Bay
Lola I.
Mandra
Kerato Pt
Nusalonga I.
Elelo
NAUTICAL MILES
5   0   5
Tatapuraka I.
Munda Bar
Munda Pt
Hubupeka I.
Koka Kate Kilivira
Tlangang Pt
Nusalavata I.
WESTERN ENT
Kuru Kuru
Tambulu I.
VILA AND MUNDA POINT AIRDROMES
NEW GEORGIA GROUP

3. Kahili and Ballale Airdomes – Bougainvile Island.

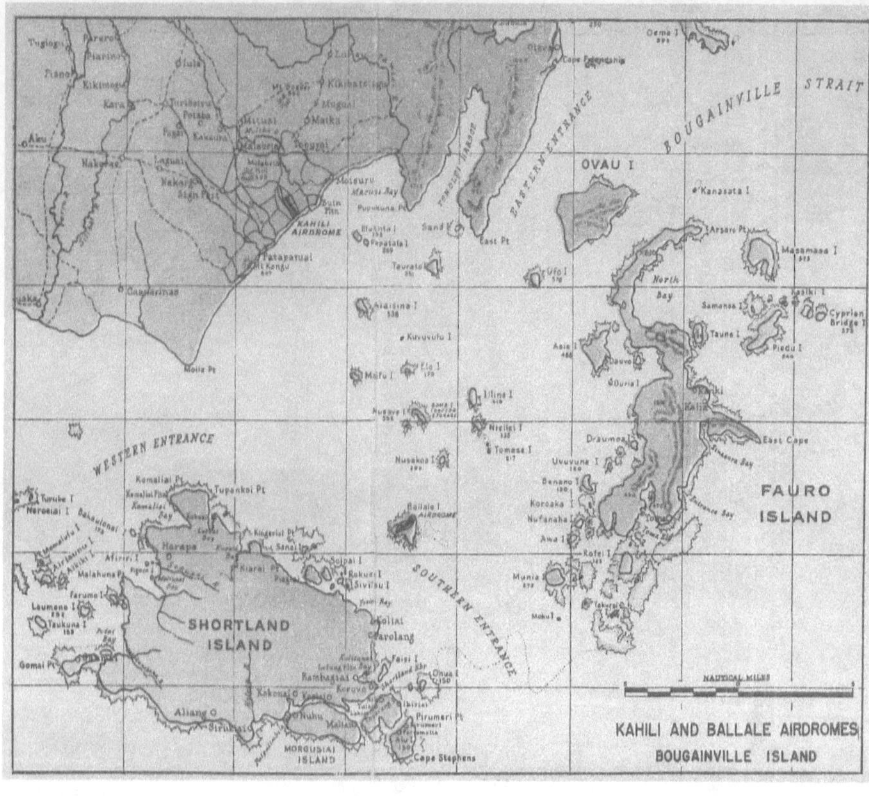

4. Buka Passage Airdrome – Buka Island.

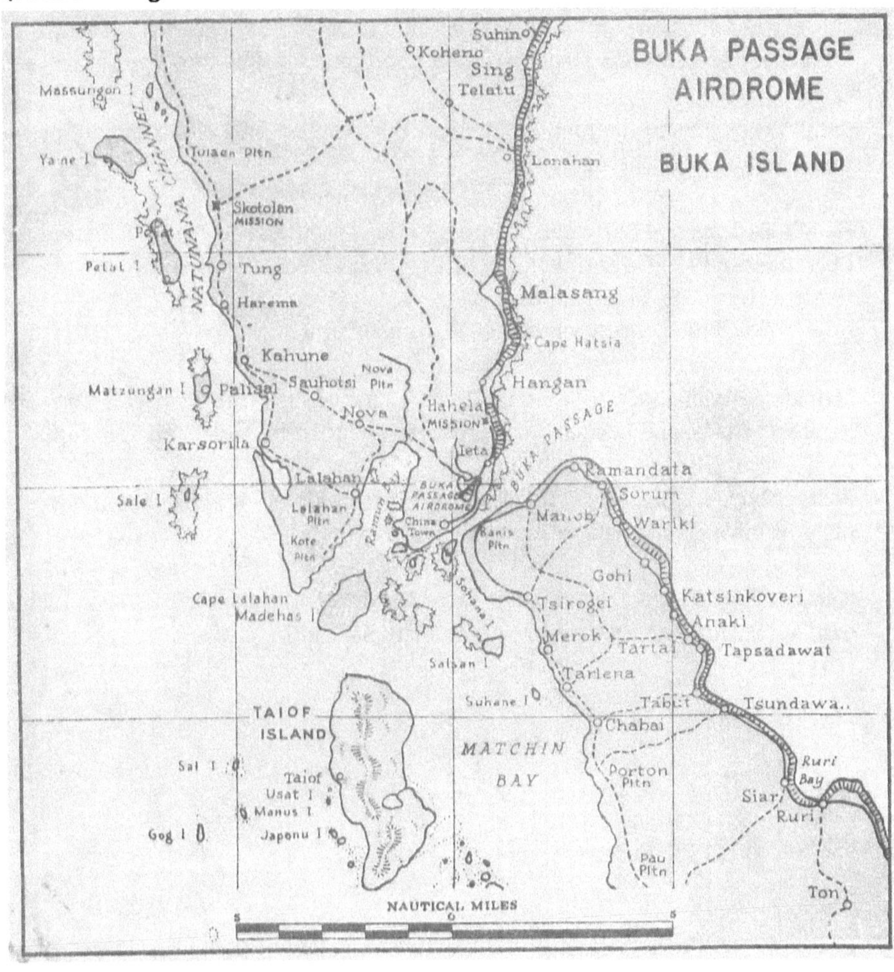

Bibliography

Altobello, Brian. *Into the Shadows Furious.* California: Presidio Press, 2000.

Craig, Berry. Hatch, Gardner, ed. *Marine Corps Aviation Association: Chronology 1912 – 1954.* Paducah, KY: Turner, 1989.

Hough, Ludwig, and Shaw. Pearl Harbor to Guadalcanal, History of U.S. Marine Corps Operations in World War II, Volume I (Historical Branch, G-3 Division, Headquarters, U.S. Marine Corps).
http://www.ibiblio.org/hyperwar/USMC/I/index.html

Livingood, William C. VMF-213 Records, including *Flight Surgeon's Logs*, Pilots Reference Maps, and Related Work Products, 1943. http://www.VMF-213.com

Richardson, C. S., ed. Diary of a Corsair Pilot in the Solomons, 1943. http://www.monongahelabooks.com/winnia.html

Wars and Conflicts of the United States Navy. Department of the Navy – Naval Historical Center. Washington, DC. http://www.history.navy.mil/